Little People, **BIG DREAMS**™

RUPAUL

Written by
Maria Isabel Sánchez Vegara

Illustrated by
Wednesday Holmes

Frances Lincoln
Children's Books

When little Ru was about to be born, a fortune-teller told his mom that her son would one day be famous. Growing up in San Diego, with his mother and three sisters, it was only a matter of time before he figured out how…

One day, his sister Renetta laid out a blanket in the backyard, took out some cookies from a paper bag and asked him to enjoy the most fabulous picnic. Ru realized we all can create magic if we try.

Playing dress-up was Ru's favorite game—and that is where he channeled his magic.

But, back in real-life, he felt like a bit of an outsider.
There were rules about how boys and girls
should look, and he didn't seem to fit in!

It was not school, but his mom who taught him
his most important lesson: do what feels right to you…

... and love yourself for who you are. Ru promised he would never stop doing all the things that made him happy.

Ru was kicked out of high school and moved to Atlanta to study performing arts. Playing with his first punk band, he mixed a prom dress with army boots on stage. Everyone wondered if he was a boy or a girl.

He was 21 when he moved to New York with his friend
Lady Bunny. Wearing a wig and a pair of heels
they showed up at every single party. They were the most
fabulous drag queens in the Lower East Side.

But drag was not only about having fun and dressing up.
For Ru, it was a way to express himself as an artist.

He mixed a spoonful of everything he loved and admired,
and put his heart into becoming the woman of his dreams.

On and offstage, Ru had found his true groove!
She felt as comfortable in high heels...

... as he did wearing his favorite pair of slippers.
It was time to share his joy and meet someone
special: his husband Georges.

Dressed as a supermodel on the catwalk, Ru released a song that was an instant success all around the world.

Soon, he was asked to be the first drag queen ever
to star in a make-up advert. And he nailed it!

Ru had his own TV and radio show, and he shared the stage with some of the most amazing artists of all time.

He even lip-synced next to his most beloved artist, Diana Ross, celebrating self-love and diversity.

All of his dreams had come true, so Ru decided to help others achieve theirs by finding America's next drag superstar. Anyone who had the courage to break free and follow their heart was welcome to the family!

Ru's show became an inspiration for thousands of lonely kids who felt that they had finally found their people.

And what's more important—a fabulous
way to celebrate who they were and what they liked.

By sharing with the world the beauty of drag, little Ru gave us valuable tips to make the most out of life:

"Don't ever think we are born just to fit in a box,
we are born to stand out."

RUPAUL

(Born 1960)

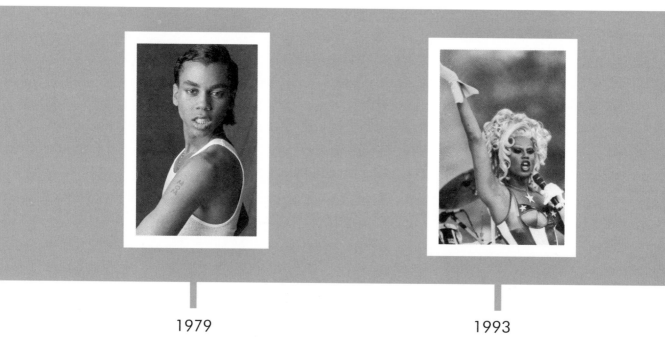

1979   1993

RuPaul Charles was born in San Diego, California, in 1960. His mother named him after roux, a key ingredient in delicious Cajun cuisine. When he was still young, his parents divorced, and little RuPaul grew up with his mother and three sisters. He was a born performer, dressing in their clothes and accessories to imitate the women he idolized, like Diana Ross and Jane Fonda. Ru found school difficult; he was expelled from one and dropped out from another. Determined to find a community he loved and that would love him back, Ru discovered an emerging culture called drag. Drag was everything he had ever dreamed of: dazzling outfits, exciting performances, and whip-smart queens with fiery personalities. The drag queens who became his friends had had tough childhoods, just like him, and RuPaul

2009

2020

finally felt understood. Soon, drag took him to New York City, where the festival Wigstock was just taking off. RuPaul danced, acted, and lip-synced his way to success. He performed in clubs, films, and music videos, and released his first hit single, 'Supermodel,' introducing the world to the magic of drag. By the end of the 1980s, he was known as the 'Queen of New York.' With a host of albums, films, and TV shows under his belt, he started the extravaganza that made him a household name: *RuPaul's Drag Race*. The TV competition gave fellow queens a chance at stardom, and became a worldwide success. Today, he remains an LGBTQ+ icon and a champion of drag culture, who shows the world that while it's one thing to look fabulous, true fierceness comes from within.

Want to find out more?

Read this great book:

The Hips on the Drag Queen Go Swish, Swish, Swish

by Lil Miss Hot Mess and Olga De Dios Ruiz

Brimming with creative inspiration, how-to projects, and useful information to enrich your everyday life, Quarto Knows is a favourite destination for those pursuing their interests and passions. Visit our site and dig deeper with our books into your area of interest: Quarto Creates, Quarto Cooks, Quarto Homes, Quarto Lives, Quarto Drives, Quarto Explores, Quarto Gifts, or Quarto Kids.

Text © 2021 Maria Isabel Sánchez Vegara. Illustrations © Wednesday Holmes 2021
Original concept of the series by Maria Isabel Sánchez Vegara, published by Alba Editorial, s.l.u
Produced under licence from Alba Editorial s.l.u and Beautifool Couple S.L.
First Published in the US in 2021 by Frances Lincoln Children's Books, an imprint of The Quarto Group.
100 Cummings Center, Suite 265D, Beverly, MA 01915, USA.
T +1 978-282-9590 www.QuartoKnows.com

ISBN 978-0-7112-4681-2
Set in Futura BT.

Published by Katie Cotton • Designed by Karissa Santos
Edited by Katy Flint • Production by Nikki Ingram
Editorial Assistance from Alex Hithersay
Manufactured In China CC022021
1 3 5 7 9 8 6 4 2

Photographic acknowledgements (pages 28-29, from left to right): 1. RuPaul photographed in photo studio, October 27, 1979 © Tom Hill/WireImage 2. Drag queen recording artist Rupaul singing into handheld mike as he performs on stage at rally festivities at Gay Rights March at the WA Monument Mall, 1993 © Robert Sherbow/The LIFE Images Collection via Getty Images 3. RuPaul takes the stage during the taping of RuPaul's Drag Race Season 2 in Culver City JULY 31, 2009 © Mark Boster/Los Angeles Times via Getty Images 4. RuPaul Charles at RuPaul's DragCon UK presented by World Of Wonder at Olympia London on January 18, 2020 in London, England © Tristan Fewings/Getty Images for World Of Wonder Productions.

MIX
Paper from responsible sources
FSC® C008047

Collect the *Little People*, **BIG DREAMS**™ series:

FRIDA KAHLO 	**COCO CHANEL**	**MAYA ANGELOU** 	**AMELIA EARHART** 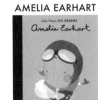	**AGATHA CHRISTIE** 	**MARIE CURIE** 
ROSA PARKS 	**AUDREY HEPBURN** 	**EMMELINE PANKHURST** 	**ELLA FITZGERALD**	**ADA LOVELACE** 	**JANE AUSTEN** 
GEORGIA O'KEEFFE 	**HARRIET TUBMAN** 	**ANNE FRANK** 	**MOTHER TERESA** 	**JOSEPHINE BAKER** 	**L. M. MONTGOMERY** 
JANE GOODALL 	**SIMONE DE BEAUVOIR** 	**MUHAMMAD ALI** 	**STEPHEN HAWKING** 	**MARIA MONTESSORI** 	**VIVIENNE WESTWOOD** 
MAHATMA GANDHI 	**DAVID BOWIE** 	**WILMA RUDOLPH** 	**DOLLY PARTON** 	**BRUCE LEE** 	**RUDOLF NUREYEV** 
ZAHA HADID 	**MARY SHELLEY**	**MARTIN LUTHER KING JR.** 	**DAVID ATTENBOROUGH** 	**ASTRID LINDGREN** 	**EVONNE GOOLAGONG** 

BOB DYLAN

ALAN TURING

BILLIE JEAN KING

GRETA THUNBERG

JESSE OWENS

JEAN-MICHEL BASQUIAT

ARETHA FRANKLIN

CORAZON AQUINO

PELÉ

ERNEST SHACKLETON

STEVE JOBS

AYRTON SENNA

LOUISE BOURGEOIS

ELTON JOHN

JOHN LENNON

PRINCE

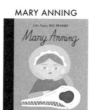

CHARLES DARWIN

CAPTAIN TOM MOORE

HANS CHRISTIAN ANDERSEN

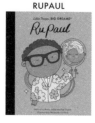

STEVIE WONDER

MEGAN RAPINOE

MARY ANNING

MALALA YOUSAFZAI

ANDY WARHOL

RUPAUL

ACTIVITY BOOKS

STICKER ACTIVITY BOOK

COLORING BOOK

LITTLE ME, BIG DREAMS JOURNAL

Discover more about the series at www.littlepeoplebigdreams.com